THE ALL NEW STYLE OF MAGAZINE-BOOKS

SDM

MP

MOCY PUBLISHING
WWW.MOCYPUBLISHING.COM

Printed by CreateSpace, An Amazon.com Company

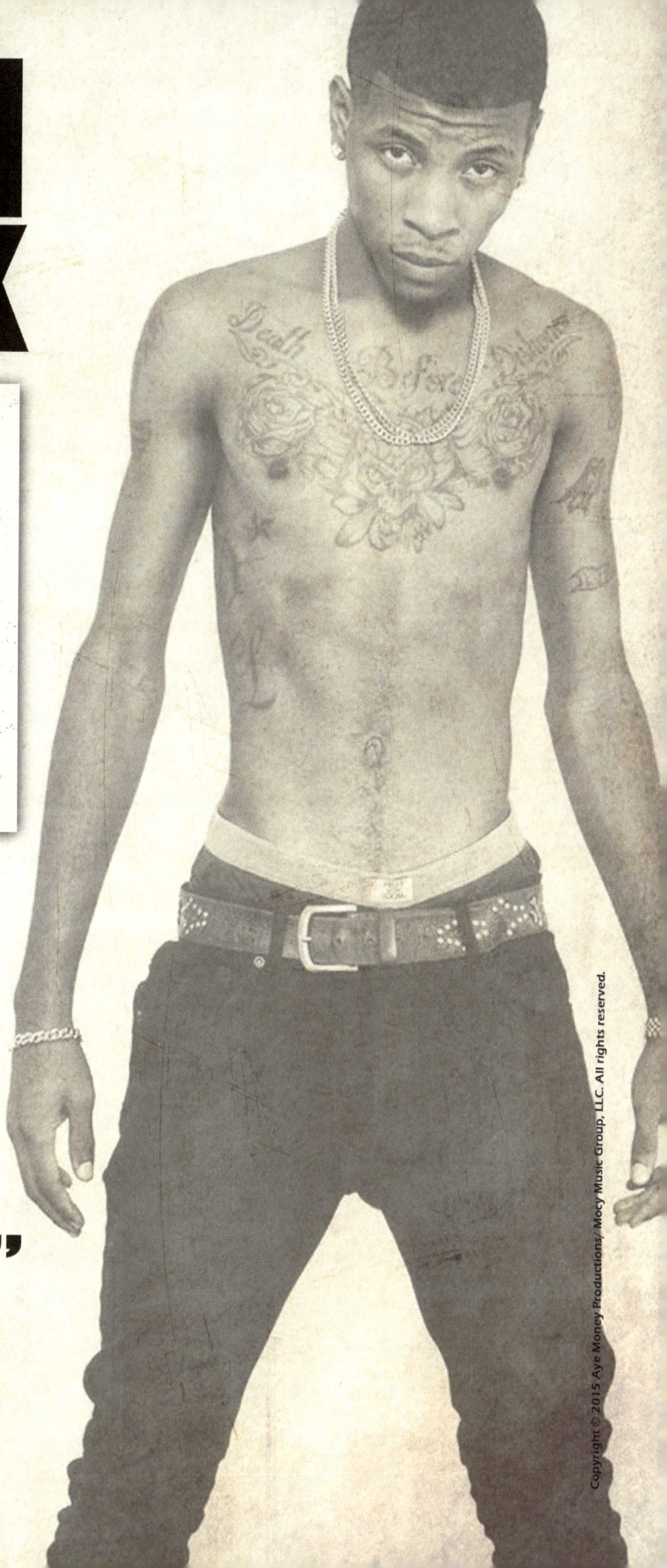

SDM

EDITOR-IN-CHIEF
D. "Casino" Bailey
casino@supportdetroitmovement.com

EDITORAL DIRECTOR
Sheree Cranford
sheree@supportdetroitmovement.com

GRAPHIC/WEB DESIGNER
D. "Casino" Bailey
casino@supportdetroitmovement.com

A&R MANAGER
Aye Money
ayemoney@supportdetroitmovement.com

ACCOUNT EXECUTIVE
Frank Harvest Jr.
frank@supportdetroitmovement.com

PHOTOGRAPHERS
David Bailey
D. "Casino" Bailey

CONTRIBUTORS
Tanya Echols
Donna Banks
Courtney Benjamin

COPY ORDERS & ADVERTISING OFFICE
Send Money Order or Check to:
Mocy Publishing
P.O. Box 35195
Detroit, Michigan 48235
(586) 646-8505
advertise@supportdetroitmovement.com

Copy Order Item #:
SDM Magazine Issue #1 2015
S&H Plus Retail Price - $9.99 per copy

WWW.SUPPORTDETROITMOVEMENT.COM

Printed by CreateSpace, An Amazon.com Company

MP
MOCY PUBLISHING

ALL NEW STREET EDITION
SDM
ISSUE 1.

Aye Money
RAPPER/PROMOTER
MAKING NOISE ALL
OVER THE MIDWEST

Mike Da Dizz
CREATING A BRAND
FOR HIMSELF WITH
THE RELEASE OF
HIS NEW VIDEO
"BOYZ IN DETROIT"

ALSO
DEJ LOAF
TAMIKO
"CHINA"
HODO
DEX OSAMA
RICH MOOK

PLUS MORE

BIG GOV
TALKS ABOUT HIS NEW ALBUM &
CONNECTIONS ON THE WEST COAST

TOP 10 CHARTS
HIGHLIGHTING THE TOP 10
RAP SINGLES OF 2015

US - $8.99

NOVEMBER 2015 No.1
WWW.SUPPORTDETROITMOVEMENT.COM

CONTENTS

16
MIKE DA DIZZ

On the road to fame sits down to talk about his new projects and how he's planning to brand the nation with his new movement.

12
AYE MONEY

Rapper/Promoter is showing new artists how to get paid and showcase their music worldwide.

20
BIG GOV

The original Black Government OG repping the D is in full swing now while launching his all new album.

23
TOP 10 CHARTS

The hottest albums and digital singles this month features Kendrick Lamar, Drake, YG, Rich Mook, Aye Money, Fetty Wap, and many more.

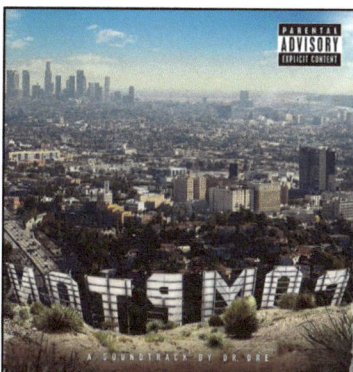

NEW ELECTRONICS

A LIST OF SOME OF THE PICK'S THIS MONTH.

BY JEFF WALKER

1 Microsoft Surface Pro 3 Tablet

Get online, watch movies and also mark up documents with the Surface Pen (included) on this tablet. It puts the Windows 10 experience at your fingertips. The 64GB of memory and microSD card slot provide options for storing your growing digital collection.

3 Bose® - SoundLink® Color Bluetooth Speaker - Black

Now enjoy clear, full-range sound you wouldn't expect from a small speaker. This speaker, durable and easy to use Bose®/SoundLink® Bluetooth speaker has voice prompts to ensure a simple Bluetooth pairing, letting you easily connect to devices.

2 Apple - iPhone 6s 16GB

A 4.7-inch Retina HD display with 3D Touch. 7000 series aluminum and stronger cover glass. An A9 chip with 64-bit desktop-class architecture. The all new 12MP iSight camera with Live Photos. Touch ID. Faster LTE and Wi-Fi. Long battery life and iOS 9 and iCloud. All in a smooth, continuous unibody design.

4 Neat - NeatDesk Premium Sheetfed Scanner - Multi

With up to 24 ppm scan speed and 600 dpi resolution, and a 50-sheet ADF (automatic document feeder), this Neat NeatDesk Premium 2005144 scanner makes it easy to keep your receipts, business cards and documents organized.

The biggest thing to happen to iPhone since iPhone.

iPhone 5 [s]

Forward thinking.

The most advanced technology all leads up to this.

iPhone 5 set a precedent, with an amazing amount of technology in a remarkably thin, light design. iPhone 5s builds on that achievement with Touch ID — a fingerprint identity sensor. An A7 chip with 64-bit architecture. An even more impressive iSight camera. And ultrafast LTE wireless.

www.apple.com

SHOTS FIRED

DEX OSAMA, DETROIT RAPPER CO-SIGNED BY MEEK MILL & DEJ LOAF, DIES AT 21 IN DETROIT AT LOCAL STRIP CLUB.

by Colin Stutz

Detroit rapper Dex Osama, who was an artist co-signed by Meek Mill and DeJ Loaf, was shot in Detroit and Died early Monday morning at a gentleman's club in Detroit.

The owner of Crazy Horse gentleman's club told Detroit station WDIV that a fight started inside his establishment around 2 AM between two groups of people, some of whom that was kicked out of the club. That's when shots were fired according to Detroit Free Press, killing Osama and injuring two other men.

Meek Mill later posted a message about Osama on Instagram, writing that he had talks with Dex about getting out of the streets and chasing his dreams. Meek Mill believed in Dex and seen him representing for Detroit.

Dex Osama also received support from his fellow rapper from Detroit DeJ Loaf, who pulled him onstage during the Summer Jamz 18 show in June. As Noisey reports, they also performed together on Oba Rowland's *"Lifestyle Part II"* remix.

Osama's start getting his street cred with his hard-

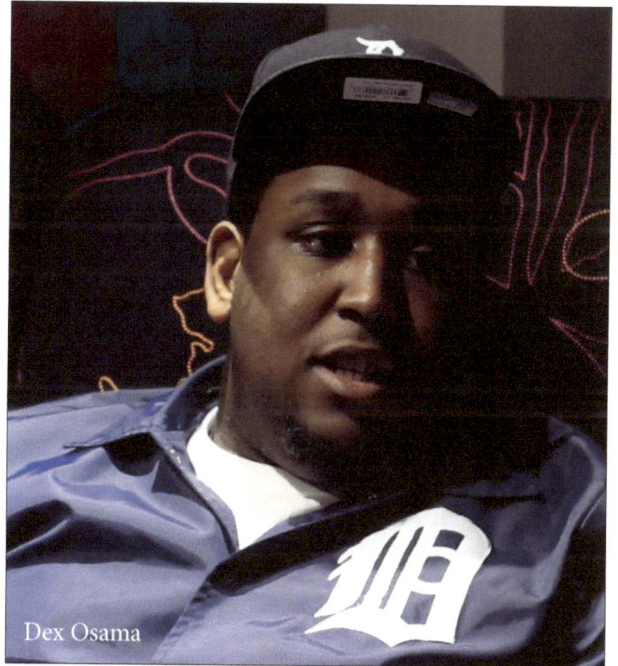
Dex Osama

core raps about Detroit street life. One of his most famous tracks, *"Death on Me,"* was a track about his mother's views about his lifestyle. Talking about how his mama said he had death on him. Words that really made Dex think about life as he knew it.

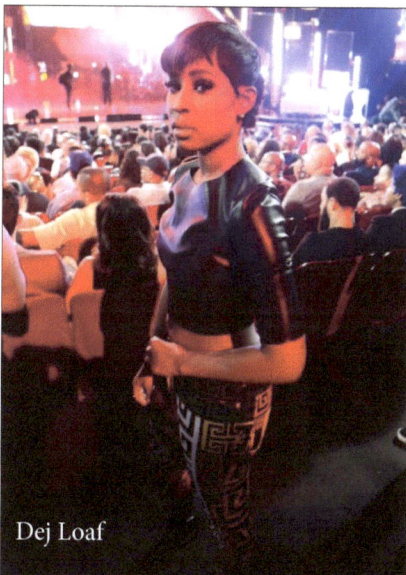
Dej Loaf

Releasing her latest EP this summer *#AndSeeThatsTheThing* has Dej Loaf on everyone's radar. Also dropping a new hit single with Big Sean called *"Back Up,"* directed by Alex Nazari shook the airwaves nationally. The video was filmed at the famous Detroit's Royal Skate Land, a roller rink Dej skated at often. Recently Dej Loaf was gracing the stage of the 2015 Hip Hop Awards

with Kid Ink, letting nothing but positive energy loose in a Detroit state of mind.

SURVIVING HARM'S WAY

IS A MOVIE LIKE PAPERBACK BOOK WRITTEN BY NOLAN "DINO" HALL
AVALIABLE ON AMAZON AND MOCYPUBLISHING.COM

by Cheraee C.

Surviving Harm's Way is a page-turning thriller and mystery. This book's plot is based on survival, greed, determination, strength, adventure, and determination. The characters in this book exemplify courage and intelligence to survive against the wilderness and military trained strangers. No matter what obstacles are thrown to the character's they find a way to prevail, and to remain loyal to each other. The ultimate goal in this book is to make it out the wilderness alive, but survival comes with costs, loss, and blessings as well. This book represents how age or size isn't nothing, but a number. The characters in this book abided by their plan of action so ultimately they were unstoppable.

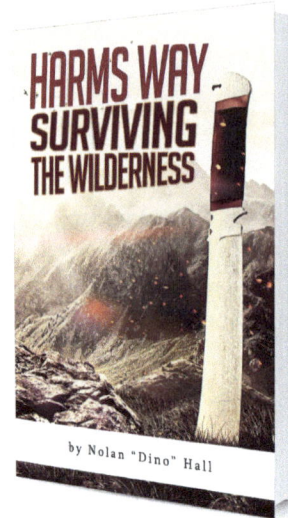

Harms Way Surviving The Wilderness
By Nolan "Dino" Hall

Available from Amazon.com and other online stores

Photography by **Casino Bailey**

AYE MONEY PROMOTIONS

RAP ARTIST/BUSINESS MAN AYE MONEY LAUNCHES A MAJOR CAMPAIGN ACROSS THE MIDWEST WITH LOCAL ARTISTS ON HOW TO GET PAID WITH THEIR MUSIC FROM GORILLA MARKETING.

by Cheraee C.

Detroit is historical for its music and remains to be a musical hub; serving ambitious artists all over the Midwest like a musical compass is Detroit's own Aye Money. Aye Money is a profound club promoter, hip hop artist, host, music publisher and manager. He is dedicated to helping artists find the right avenues they need to publicize their music and advancing in the music industry. Aye Money's love for music motivated him to start his own business Aye Money Promotions and Publishing LLC in 2015.

Aye Money has a multitude of resources to assist artists with promoting their music. Some of those resources include him utilizing his radio and club connections, helping artists get their music out to the public on iTunes, Amazon, and other online music stores, and helping artists publish their music. Most importantly, he helps artists receive royalties from their music from YouTube videos, downloads, music streams, different music apps, and more by helping them get affiliated with a Performing Rights Organization (PRO). These companies are responsible for collecting income on behalf of songwriters and music publishers. Also, Aye Money signs artists to his company and has signed many local Detroit artists. Lastly, Aye Money has showcases at the Bullfrog where he's the host every 2nd and 4th Sunday giving artists chances to win live interview spots on Hot 107.5 fm in Detroit, MI.

Aye Money is a diplomat of the Support Detroit Movement. The movement is a division of Aye Money Promotions and Publishing LLC and Mocy Music Publishing LLC. Furthermore, Aye Money has (SDM) t-shirts and a (SDM) compilation album where local artists have an opportunity to get a slot on the album. Please visit supportdetroitmovement.com for more information on how to submit your music for the next compilation album and stay connected with Aye Money because he is a talented force who has many projects underway highlighting Detroit music. His next power move is coming out with a Support Detroit Movement DVD.

Bullfrog Night Club
Detroit, MI

MR. MARK HUNTER

FROM THE STREETS TO THE STAGE MARK HUNTER MAKES A REMARKABLE TURNAROUND WITH HIS LIFE TO NOW BECOMING A PLAYWRIGHT, AUTHOR, AND PRODUCER.

by Cheraee C.

Arising from a lifestyle of drugs, fatal experiences, and street afflictions is a dexterous man who is prone to be on a TV or a center stage near you. Mark Hunter is a very savvy playwright, author, and producer who is transforming into a literary powerhouse. He has undertaken many ventures with the godfather of urban theatre Mr. Shelly Garrett who produced the hit stage play "Beauty Shop."

Thankful to have survived the streets, there are so many scenarios where Mark's journey could've ended. It was one very distinctive experience he recalls in his troublesome past that sparked his ambitions. The moment of clarity for Mark is when he realized that his street dreams were just barricading his real dreams and his God-given gifts. Now Mark has a long list of accomplishments and blessings on top of blessings.

Mark's street experiences has revived his desire to write. In 2008, Mark started his own business called Remarkable Productions. In 2012, he produced his 1st stage play *"Eyes of Deception."* Mark has also started a non-profit organization called ReMarkable Men where he mentors young men.

Mr. ReMarkable has worked with some big names including Jackie Christie from Basketball Wives LA, Cocoa Brown, Tony Terry, Christian Keyes, Cuba Gooding Sr and so many others as he travels the world determined to make a name for himself. Mark has been featured on Oprah's Network on the Raising Whitley show. He has produced a variety of plays, is a promotional tourist, and is setting the bar for playwrights in Detroit.

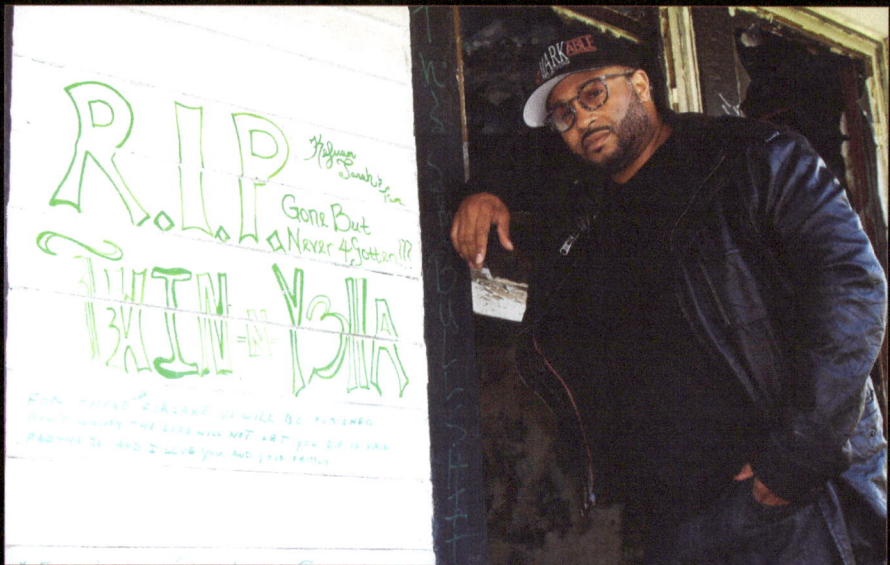

Trying to be successful is the hardest thing Mark has ever done. The proximity of many friendships and relationships has been varying. The quest of success has a way of changing the people that surround you. Trying to maintain his credibility in this business is another challenge that Mark is dealing with. You never know what roads you're going to be on, so life is a cycle where you have to restructure continually and rebuild. Success doesn't come easy and it certainly isn't going to come without taking risks.

Presently, Mark is working on a reality show, and a novel/memoir called Flipping the Script, and a movie that will have debuts in 2016. In March 2016, Mark will be dropping another hit stage play called "Let it Burn" as well. You can stay hip to his upcoming projects and events by visiting his new website www.officiallyremarkable.com.

BLACK RAIN

TALKS ABOUT HOW HE BEGIN HIS CAREER AS A YOUTH AND HOW HE GREW INTO A PROFESSIONAL MUSIC ARTIST WHILE WORKING ON HIS NEW ALBUM " FRESH OFF THE RUNWAY".

by Donna Banks

Michael Flowers as known as Black Rain was born on May 19th, 1982. He grew up on the west side of Detroit raised by both parents. During his childhood he listen to different genres of music from artists such as The Funkadelic's, Pink Floyd, The Rolling Stones and NWA. He gives credit to his father and uncle for that exposure cause him to fall in love with music but he ultimately fell in love with the creativity and the lyrical word play of hip-hop.

His early experimentation with music bought him to a place of uncertainty, he couldn't decide which avenue he wanted to take and took a sabbatical from music. Some years later, the intriguing sound of a cipher going on in a crowded lunchroom caught his attention. It was at that moment his love for hip-hop was rekindled. Despite his love for hip-hop being rekindled, it still took a backseat to the hustle. In 2005, the street life almost got the best of him. He then decided to remove himself from the street life and live freely and make his love for music known to the world.

In 2006, he started the journey to reconcile his life and fulfill his dreams. The birth of *"The Bad Guys"* a group that included him, Killa Kev, General Beans, and Philly Fresh worked diligently to record 'Bad News The Mix Tape'. The mixtape was independently sold around the city with hopes of building an audience and eventually being the next big thing. Shortly after 'Bad News' hit the streets the group was dismantled, but Rain decided to continue with his journey to become a star!!!

With the advice of Killa Kev, he decided to become a writer. In a matter of months he wrote 18 songs which he's currently in the studio recording new songs weekly. He has toured in different states, currently has songs in rotation, radio interview and recently released his first mixtape *"Rain Organics"* and is currently working on

material for the upcoming CD *"Fresh Off The Runway"*. You can follow him on Facebook @ Michael Black Rain Flowers. on Instagram @therealblackrain or Twitter @ realblackrain. Also watch for a new album soon.

MIKE
DA DIZZ

SELF-MADE MIKE DA DIZZ

IS ONE OF THE HOTTEST RAPPERS IN THE MIDWEST. HE'S BEEN ON THE BLOCK BANGING OUT HIT RECORDS AND VIDEOS FOR SOME TIME NOW. HE'S NOW READY TO GO WORLDWIDE.

Photography by Mike Da Dizz

MIKE DA DIZZ has been a local artist from the Detroit rap scene since 2003. He's worked with some of Detroit legends like Stretch Money, Team Eastside Peezy & Maserati Money. He's also performed at some of the biggest gigs like the Legendary Masonic Temple in Detroit, MI. Mike Da Dizz recently released his hot new single titled *"You Mad Feat. Nuke"* that have the streets talking and a lot of social gangsters upset, angry or as they chant in the Song (Oh You Mad Bruh). He's presently working on his EP titled *"I'M DONE TALKING".* The name of this EP speaks for its self. Mike said the he feels he's Under Rated and needs more respect in the industry.

You can see Mike Da Dizz performing Live with Diggy Simmons, Lil George and Neisha Neshae at the Music Hall in Detroit, Michigan November 21, 2015.

Thanks S/O: Thanks to Mocy Music for this opportunity and support, I would like to thank all my supporters, friends, family, and coworkers, they keep me happy. Gotta s/o a special thanks to my wife and son for giving me nothing but motivation. To all my bros the ones staying true and loyal. To my Momma, she hit me up with some cash and said "This is for your music", that was my green light to go. And last but never least, (God), its great to have a Father in your corner continuously giving you a shoulder to lean on, and when I'm down he reaches his hand out to pull me thru that Window Of Success.

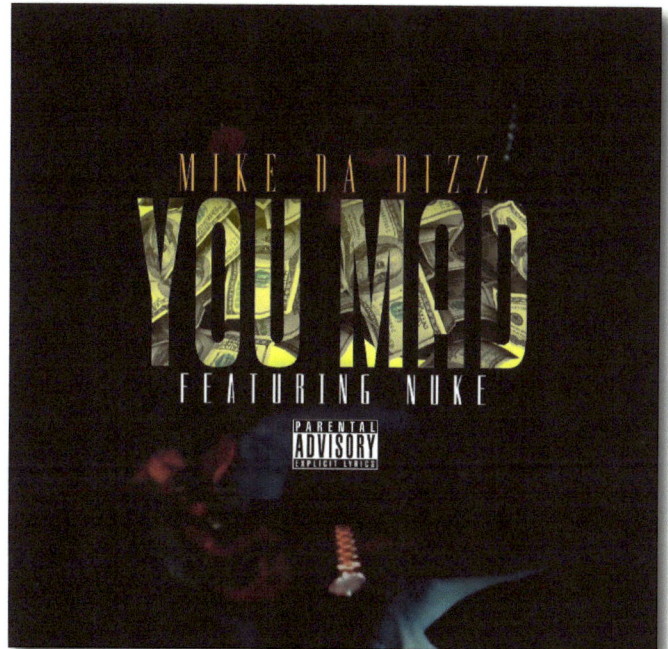

Instagram & Twitter: @Mikedadizz416
Facebook: Mike Da Dizz

MORE MONEY

BMI ANNOUNCES HOW THEY WILL START REWARDING MORE ROYALTIES FOR MUSIC STREAMING.

by Cheraee C.

BMI
Valuing music since 1939.

Serving music by the masses from all arenas of the globe, the company BMI is reinventing itself by creating a new valuation system strictly for the hottest played songs on digital markets such as Spotify and Rhapsody. The first step to improving royalty distribution is to give BMI songwriters and publishers who are in the top 20% bracket a Streaming Hits Bonus.

Even though, BMI has made a similar bonus for the most played songs in contemporary music; this new bonus has new benefits and advantages that expand on the digital trends in today's society. The beauty of this new incentive is to open doors for songwriters and publishers who might not receive radio bonuses. Dedicated to improving royalty distributions, BMI will constantly propose new strategies that surround this bonus.

As technology expands, BMI will continue to maximize the roles that music plays in its business digitally and physically and ensure that all parties are accounted for and equally represented.

THE ORIGINAL BIG GOV

AN ORIGINAL OG OF STREET MUSIC BIG GOV GIVING US HIS THOUGHTS ON WHY MOST ARTIST FELL AT THE GAME AND HOW HE LOVES HIS WEST COAST CONNECTIONS.

by Cheraee C.

Originating from southwest Detroit is lyricist, rapper, and producer "Big Gov." Besides pursuing his rap career, Big Gov is a full time dad and has a 9-5. With 30 years up under his rap belt he is steady mobbing the rap game with his persistence and resilience. Currently working on a four part album, Big Gov just released part one to the 4-part album collection titled *"No Signs of Weakness."* His favorite part of his upcoming album is the intro which features a voicemail from his mother who passed away February 2005.

Family is a distinctive variable that has influenced Big Gov musically. One song of significance to him is a song titled *"Legendary Genes"* which features his son Lil Gov. This track reflects on how Big Gov inspires his son or any artist to make music from the heart.

Fundamentally, Big Gov feels the rap game is premature because artists aren't making real music anymore. Nowadays an artist rather be an one hit wonder then a legend. Artists should be focused on longevity and making classic music; music you can still feel 40 years from now. Nowadays artists are too busy faking or duplicating their image to even be labeled as a real artist. In Big Gov's opinion the real artists include artists who are undiscovered and overlooked. Being a veteran in the game, Big Gov plans to advocate for new talent so that the future of rap music isn't continuously misconstrued by greed or entertainment

Big Gov has many connections on the West Coast. From the Bay Area to L,A,, Big Gov's fans know how to show him some California Love. Selling out a concert on the West Coast is easier then selling out a concert in his own hometown. In the West Coast lies a different breed of fans where Big Gov's music Is notable, respected, and in high-demand. A lot of people in Detroit have preset attitudes that conflicts their interest to show others support. The West Coast is a place where you can connect and network with some of the biggest names in the business. The West Coast appreciates artists like Big Gov whose grind don't stop and music amplifies real hip hop.

Whatever happened to rappers like Big Gov who based their raps on real-life stories? With music galore, and new and improved projects underway, Big Gov is a talented Detroit source of rap you have to stay connected too.

ALL NEW STREET EDITION

SDM

ISSUE 1.

Aye Money

RAPPER/PROMOTER MAKING NOISE ALL OVER THE MIDWEST

Mike Da Dizz

CREATING A BRAND FOR HIMSELF WITH THE RELEASE OF HIS NEW VIDEO "BOYZ IN DETROIT"

BIG GOV

TALKS ABOUT HIS NEW ALBUM & CONNECTIONS ON THE WEST COAST

TOP 10 CHARTS

HIGHLIGHTING THE TOP 10 RAP SINGLES OF 2015

US - $8.99
00899 >

9 781940 831091

NOVEMBER 2015 No.1
WWW.SUPPORTDETROITMOVEMENT.COM

TOP 10 CHARTS

TOP 10 DIGITAL SINGLES AND ALBUMS
NOVEMBER 1, 2015

TOP 10 CHARTS

DRAKE - BREAKING RECORDS ON THE CHARTS WITH HIS NEW SINGLE "HOTLINE BLING".

SDM TOP 10 SINGLES CHART OF THE MONTH

No.	Artist - Song Title
1	DRAKE - HOTLINE BLING
2	DEJ LOAF - ME U & HENNESSY FT. LIL WAYNE
3	RICH MOOK - YES I DO
4	KENDRICK LAMAR - ALRIGHT
5	ESKO - NEW WAVE
6	JIDENNA - CLASSIC MAN FT. ROMAN GIANARTHUR
7	YG - WHO DO YOU LOVE
8	MIKE DA DIZZ - BOYZ IN DETROIT
9	KING DILLON - LOOK AT DAT FT. KING DILLON & 2K VELL
10	FETTY WAP - MY WAY

SDM TOP 10 ALBUMS CHART OF THE MONTH

No.	Artist - Album Title
1	KENDRICK LAMAR - TO PIMP A BUTTERFLY
2	DRAKE & FUTURE - WHAT A TIME TO BE ALIVE
3	DR. DRE - COMPTON
4	JP ONE - FIRE AND BRIMSTONE II
5	BIG GOV - NO SIGNS OF WEAKNESS
6	THE WEEKEND - BEAUTY BEHIND THE MADNESS
7	FETTY WAP - FETTY WAP
8	KOSTA - D.I.Y.
9	AYE MONEY - SUPPORT DETROIT MOVEMENT COMPILATION (VOLUME 1)
10	UNV - UNV

Compton

ARTIST: Dr. Dre
REVIEWER: Cheraee C.
RATING: 4

TOP 3 ALBUMS THIS MONTH

It's been a 14-year-gap since Dr. Dre released a studio album, but now the Aftermath rapper has dropped his third album he calls "Compton." Dr. Dre's net worth is reportedly about 700 million so in all honesty, Dr. Dre has enough income circulating around his other businesses that he doesn't need to make albums. The album "Compton" is a soundtrack that coincides with the movie "Straight Outta Compton" in which Dr. Dre played a role in producing it. The album as well as the movie pays tribute to Dre's hometown Compton, and his NWA roots.

The album "Compton" made top 2 on Billboard Charts in it's first week so the album was pretty genius. A collective number of strong hip hop artists are featured on the album including Kendrick Lamar, Ice Cube, Snoop Dogg, Eminem, and an A-list of others. The track list on this album is very impressive and precise as this album was thoroughly planned and recorded, and each track creates moments from experiences that are deeper then the rap itself. It's nothing like a rapper mogul who can make a comeback into the music industry and still be buzz-worthy.

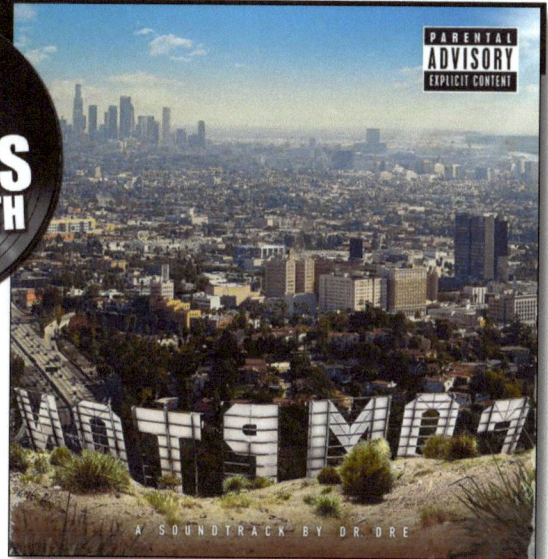

RATE METER: 1 - WACK   2 - NEEDS WORK   3 - STRAIGHT 4 - BANGER 5 - CLASSIC

D.I.Y.

ARTIST: Kosta
REVIEWER: Frank Holver
RATING: 4

Released exclusively first on Apple Music and iTunes, the new album by Kosta slowly start climbing the chart. Kosta brings back real hip hop and street rap that we can all remember. On his one track "Lottery" Kosta draws a picture on how things would go once his album goes viral. And after listening to the album he's definitely on his on his way to platinum.

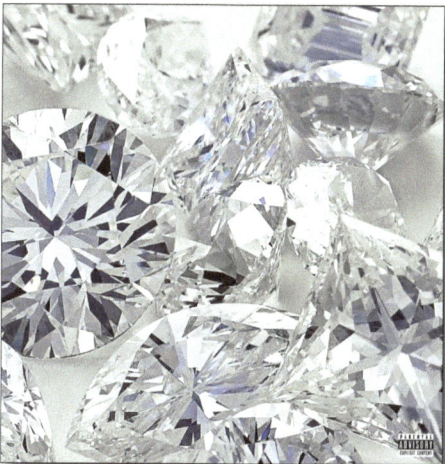

What a Time To Be Alive

ARTIST: Drake & Future
REVIEWER: Cheraee C.
RATING: 4

A fresh, trendy collaborative from two of the illest MC's in the music industry who both recently dropped very successful, chart topping albums. This album musically and lyrically entails two rappers who can rap and vocally challenge their audience with catchy, unforgettable lyrics.

HEELS & SKILLZ

Marissa

is a very sexy bartender from Detroit, MI. Her favorite hobbies are being a full-time mother, volleyball and going to the gun range.

instagram
@ms_pershard

Photo by
Casino Bailey

HEELS &
SKILLZ

Donna Banks

is an EMT First responder, entertainment manager, and part-time model from Detroit, MI. Her favorite hobbies are shopping, traveling, music and sports.

instagram
@MSBANKSBBE

Photo by
Brian Williams

STREET TALK

TAMIKO "CHINA" HODO FROM THE DETROIT STREETS TO THE FEDS.
by Cheraee C.

Tamiko "China" Hodo

Incarcerated at a federal medical correctional facility in Kentucky is Tamiko "China" Hodo. Labeled on the street as China Boss with connections from Detroit to LA. China was charged and convicted of conspiracy involving an excess of 1,000 kilograms of marijuana, five kilos of cocaine, and 280 grams of crack cocaine. Her sentence was later reduced for her small involvement in the case. The case also involved her ex-boyfriend Orlando Gordon which is London "Deelishis" Charles as we say in the hood "baby daddy." China is expected to touch down in a few years, but not without holding down her street cred for not snitching.

China is well missed by her community because she was also a provider in her neighborhood throwing events including kids clothing giveaways, food drives, and baby showers for single mothers. She was also the manager for Detroit's own erotic rap artist Jai'Laye. As said by China, "this experience was something I needed. I'm going to take life a lot different the next time around."

NEXT 2 BLOW

MR. "YES I DO" RICH MOOK
DROPS A HIT RECORD ACROSS
THE NATION AND ONLINE

Steaming from the Brightmo streets in Detroit is a smoking hot, independent artist who goes by the name of Rich Mook. Apart from rapping Rich Mook is steady evolving as an actor, a model, a barber, an artist, and a director. Music is hereditary for Mook who was inspired by his iconic aunt Teisha Brown who sings with the legendary group Brownstown as well as people encouraging him to take a walk of faith in music.

His road to stardom has been rocky, but rewarding because Mook understands you have to put miles on your success. Detroit might be a metropolis city, but not metropolis enough for a record deal. If it wasn't for Mook traveling from coast to coast, networking, doing shows and promos, he wouldn't have manufactured the connections and the opportunities he has made for himself. No matter what the interval of time it takes Mook to reach fame, he isn't looking for no handouts, and is a certified dream chaser.

Consistently, Mook lives in the studio dropping mixtapes back to back. In 2012, he released his first mixtape The Come Up hosted by DJ Pest who is a prominent DJ and a musical generator in Detroit. Also, Rich Mook works very closely with DJ Pest and DJ Pest's company Team Hustler. Presently, Mook is gearing up for the release of his fourth mixtape "Doubt Kills" set to drop sometime in November. Rich Mook's single "Yes I Do" is a street banger that got the internet going crazy. Through his music, Rich Mook plays with different styles and sounds, he tells stories from real life experiences, and he makes versatile music from hardcore hip hop to turn-up music.

For bookings email Rich Mook at richmookbookings@gmail.com. As Mook quotes "grind and do what you don't want to do now so you can see and live life how you dreamed of in the future.

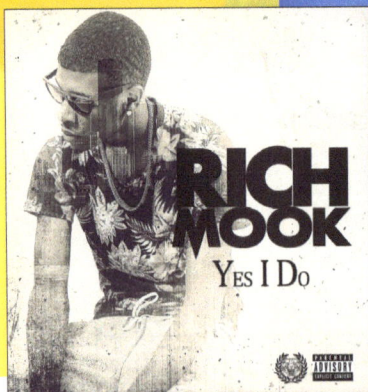

Rich Mook - Yes I Do
(Aye Money Productions/Mocy Music Group)

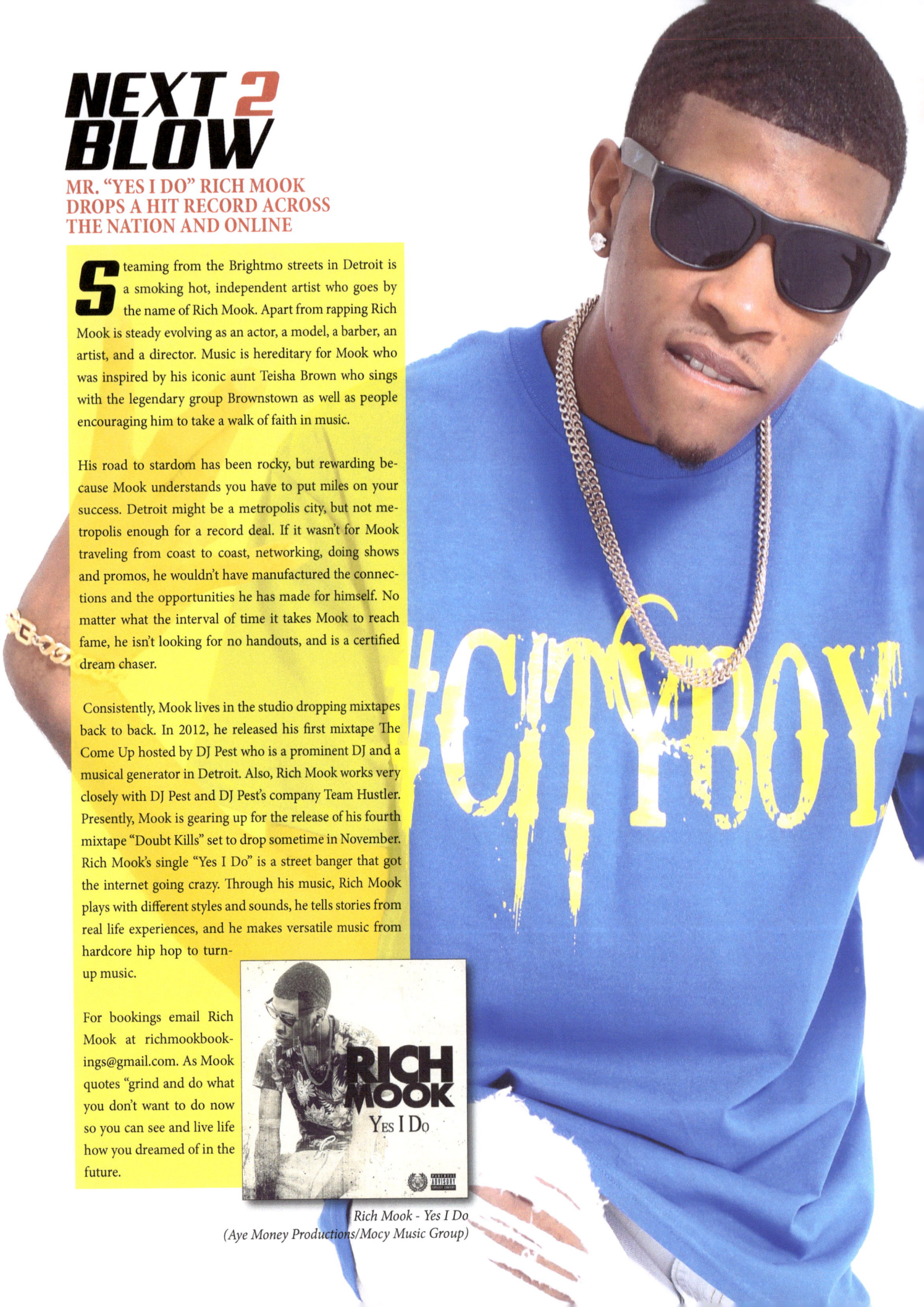

Taking the streets by storm is an independent artist from the west side of Detroit is FreshMen ENT's very own AStreetz.

The struggle is real to be a paramount artist, but AStreetz refuses to have standstill ambition. Constantly, at the peak of his relevance he's spitting bars in the studio, crafting new music, performing at shows, and shooting new videos. Despite not having a dream team, management, and being his main investor, Astreetz is not letting nothing knock his hustle. Astreetz isn't no typical artist and intends to exemplify that Detroit artists are versatile and don't just have one similar sound.

On 10/06/15 AStreetz released his latest mixtape *ROSE Vol. 2* which is an acronym for the Return of Something Extraordinary. His mixtape is available on Google Play, Spotify, Tidal, and all major online music distributors. AStreetz' debut single *"Focused"* is a smooth street banger and is available on YouTube and Soundcloud. His mixtape features various Detroit artists and singers including Asianae, Stephon Johnson, and Neisha Neshae. Another track banger from the mixtape is entitled *"Real Talk"* as it sheds light on his life from his childhood experiences to being a father. Its nothing like making soulful music that everybody can relate to.

You can find AStreetz on Soundcloud @astreetz, on Twitter and

AStreetz

IG @astreetz313, and on Facebook @ AStreetzFreshMenLawson.

Stay tuned to the journey of AStreetz because he is determined to rep his city, and has many projects in the making.

King Ron

Evolving from delinquent chronicles, fresh into music airwaves is the east side Detroit artist King Ron. King Ron has been rapping since he was nine years old and has been actively pursuing his musical artistry since 2011. A song from King Ron is like reading a page from an urban best-selling novel as he uses his music to paint vivid, mental pictures. In relation to Detroit music, King Ron describes his sound as foreign.

King Ron's debut single *"Pandemonium"* featuring Icewood Vezzo is available on YouTube, iTunes, and pressplay.com. Hitting the streets mid-November is King Ron's first mixtape Future Millionaire which will be the start of a series of mixtapes. Another track from the mixtape is a song called *"Dreams and Wishes"* where King Ron taps into his past and shares his story with the world. Some hot features from the mixtape include Detroit artists Rico Will, Luwee V. Stunna, and Danny Mellz. His mixtape was exclusively produced by TheRealWhiteMike, MStaxx, and BreadBoi Foe.

Destined for greatness, King Ron is aiming on a successful single, a successful mixtape, releasing an EP, and eventually having his first live concert in his hometown. To listen to King Ron's music you can find him on Soundcloud, IG, Twitter, and Google @darealkingron, and Facebook @Ron King.

SNAP
SHOTS

Email Your Snap Shots to
snapshots@supportdetroitmovement.com

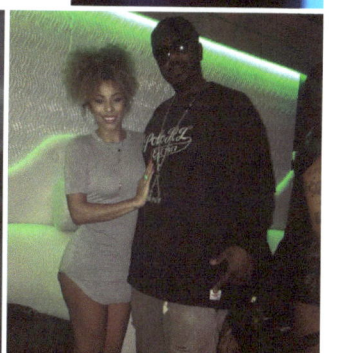

GET CASH INSTANTLY
NOW BUSINESSES CAN GET THEIR CASH FROM CUSTOMERS
INSTANTLY WITHOUT THE 1-3 DAY WAIT WITH SQUARE

by Casino B.

Now, when you sell with Square, you can deposit your funds in seconds with Instant Deposit*. Once you swipe or key in the card information manually, just click on the Activity menu on the App and click on the instant deposit button, giving yourself faster access to your cash to cover expenses, pay employees, and grow your business. Deposits can be made anytime—even late at night and on weekends and holidays.

Each deposit costs 1% of the total deposit amount. That's it. All account balances greater than $50 and less than $2,500 are eligible for Instant Deposit.

Instant Deposit enables you to deposit your balance immediately—any time, any day. To make an instant deposit, just tap the three horizontal lines at the top-left corner of the Register app, then tap Activity.

* Instant Deposit is available for most debit cards. Funds are usually available in seconds, but are subject to your bank's availability schedule.

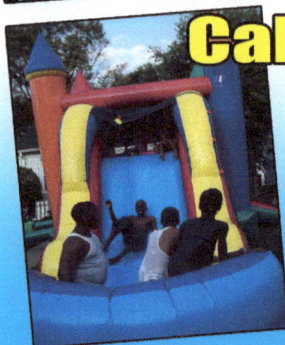

THE ALL NEW STYLE OF MAGAZINE-BOOKS

www.ingramcontent.com/pod-product-compliance
Lightning Source LLC
Chambersburg PA
CBHW040020050426
42452CB00002B/64